When Words Won't Come

By Leah Adams

Scripture marked (ESV): *The Holy Bible, English Standard Version,* copyright © 2001 by Crossway Bibles, a division of Good News Publishers. Used by permission. All rights reserved.

Scripture marked *The Message* (MSG): Copyright ©1 993, 1994, 1995, 1996, 2000, 2001, 2002 by Eugene H. Peterson.

Scripture marked (NASB): *New American Standard Bible* (NASB), Copyright © 1960, 1962, 1963, 1968, 1971, 1972, 1973, 1975, 1977, 1995 by The Lockman Foundation Used by permission. All rights reserved.

Scripture marked (NCV) – *The Holy Bible, New Century Version*®. Copyright © 2005 by Thomas Nelson, Inc. Used by permission. All rights reserved.

Scripture marked (NIV): *Holy Bible, New International Version.* NIV®. Copyright © 1973, 1978, 1984 by International Bible Society. Used by permission of Zondervan Publishing House.

Scripture marked (NKJV): *The Holy Bible, New King James Version.* Copyright © 1982 by Thomas Nelson, Inc. Use by permission. All rights reserved.

Scripture marked (NLT): *Holy Bible, New Living Translation,* copyright © 1996, 2004, 2007, 2011 by Tyndale House Foundation. Used by permission of Tyndale House Publishers, Inc. Carol Stream, Illinois 60188. All rights reserved.

Published by Warner Press, Inc, Anderson, IN 46012

Warner Press and "WP" logo is a trademark of Warner Press, Inc

Copyright ©2013 by Warner Press Inc

All rights reserved

No part of this publication may be reproduced, stored in a retrieval system, or transmitted in any form or by any means—electronic, mechanical, photocopy, recording, or any other method of storage—except for brief quotations in printed reviews, without the prior permission of the publisher.

ISBN: 978-1-59317-708-9

Author: Leah Adams

Editor: Karen Rhodes

Cover by Curtis D. Corzine

Design and layout: Curtis D. Corzine

Printed in the USA

Deuteronomy 30:19

Today I have given you the choice between life and death, between blessings and curses. I call on heaven and earth to witness the choice you make. Oh, that you would choose life, that you and your descendants might live!

Deuteronomy 30:19 (NLT)

This verse seems to be a no-brainer at first blush. *Who wouldn't choose life over death? What person in their right mind would choose curses over blessings?*

The reasonable next questions are: What choices bring life and blessings? What choices bring death and curses?

Life and blessings choices: Follow God. Obey God. Love God. Allow the Holy Spirit to live through you. Live with character and integrity. Walk in holiness. Share Jesus with other people.

Death and curses: Do your own thing. Treat God as if He is not important. Live to please yourself (selfish). Make poor character choices. Engage in profanity, adultery, lying, cheating, stealing, and immodest dress. Abuse your body through food, drugs, and alcohol.

Hmmm, which are you choosing?

You may be thinking, *"What I do is my own business. It doesn't affect anyone but me."*

Au, contraire! Glance back at the last part of the verse above. ***"Choose life, THAT YOU AND YOUR DESCENDANTS MAY LIVE."*** We are talking children, grandchildren, great grands, etc. Your choices today will directly impact your family tomorrow and decades in the future.

Heaven and earth are waiting. What will be your choice? Life and blessing? Death and curses? You must choose wisely.

Psalm 56:8

Does your heart ache for those who are going through difficult times? Perhaps you are the one walking a difficult path. This life is full of hurts and tragedies, but God offers us a bit of encouragement for the hurting heart in Psalms.

> You keep track of all my sorrows. You have collected all my tears in your bottle. You have recorded each one in your book.
>
> Psalm 56:8 (NLT)

In this verse, God enters into our sorrows, hurts and pain. He keeps track of the things that make us weep and records them in a book. He reaches down, just like a loving parent, and wipes away our tears with His gentle Father-hand, tenderly placing each tear in a bottle.

Why in the world would God collect our tears and place them in a bottle? The Bible promises that those who sow in tears will reap in joy. Perhaps each stored tear will be poured out of that bottle by God, as a heaping helping of joy when we reach heaven.

Our Father, our Daddy, our Abba, pays attention to us. He is not a far-off and distant God, but one who is close enough to gather our tears in a heavenly bottle. So, the next time you weep, know that God is storing up your tears in heaven.

Isaiah 41:10

Fear.

We are a fear-saturated, fear-driven people.

Don't believe it?

- We fear growing old, so we exercise and put on all sorts of creams to make us more youthful.
- We fear heights, so we keep our feet firmly planted on terra firma.
- We fear being alone, so we surround ourselves with people and activities.
- We fear being ridiculed, so we do everything we can to fit in.

God offers us a word of encouragement and comfort in Isaiah 41:10:

So don't worry, because I am with you. Don't be afraid, because I am your God. I will make you strong and will help you; I will support you with my right hand that saves you. (NCV)

Don't panic. I'm with you. There's no need to fear for I'm your God. I'll give you strength. I'll help you. I'll hold you steady, keep a firm grip on you. (The Message)

This comes after "Why does fear overtake us? Could it be we don't really understand **Who** our God is?

God is the Creator of all that exists.

- …the sustainer of life, yes, your life.
- …the source of all wisdom and knowledge.
- …the One to whom Satan answers.
- …the Knower of every deep and secret thing.
- …the One who appoints leaders and authorities…and takes them out of power.
- …your Protector and Defender.
- …the Sender of the lightening, rain and snow .
- …the Watcher over every sparrow that falls…and flies.
- …the One Who loves you more than you can ever fathom.

So, dear friend, do not be afraid!

Nehemiah 9:7-8

How do you rate on the *faithfulness scale*? Do you find it easy to be faithful to God in the good times, but more difficult when times are hard? *You are not alone.*

In Nehemiah 9:7-8 (NKJV), God offers us a word about faithfulness through the example of Abraham:

> *You are the Lord God, Who chose Abram, And brought him out of Ur of the Chaldeans, And gave him the name Abraham; You found his heart faithful before You, And made a covenant with him To give the land of the Canaanites, The Hittites, the Amorites, The Perizzites, the Jebusites, And the Girgashites—To give it to his descendants. You have performed Your words, For You are righteous.*

Consider these seven words: "You found his heart faithful before you."

Does God see your heart as faithful toward Him? What a question!

Has it occurred to you that a faithful heart is not necessarily a perfect heart?

Abraham was not perfect. He blew it a few times and in big ways. Yet something in his heart caused God to see him as faithful.

Do you find encouragement in that fact or have you fallen prey to the thinking that if you mess up, even in the smallest thing, you are a failure? Do you feel as if God could never look at you and call you faithful?

Take heart, friend. Hear God say, "I see your heart. I know you desire to please Me even when you don't get it 100% right. I call you faithful."

Hebrews 10:35

Hebrews 10:35 (NKJV):

> *Therefore do not cast away your confidence, which has a great reward.*

Seems like a non-descript little verse, huh? NOT! It packs a powerful punch. See that word "confidence"? The original Greek word means something pretty special. It is a word that pertains specifically to our spoken words as we share the message of the gospel. The idea the writer of Hebrews is trying to communicate is that we can be bold and confident as we share the message of salvation because of the cross of the Christ.

This word means that as a believer in Jesus Christ, you have blood-bought confidence that says "go out there and be Jesus to the world." It assures you that you have the hope and boldness you need to speak up for Him. Even better, it means that when you come up against something that really tests your faith, you can be confident that you will be equipped and enabled to walk through it and come forth as gold.

So, do not throw away, discard, or discount your confidence. You are enabled and equipped through the blood of Jesus Christ and the indwelling Holy Spirit to walk out this faith journey in victory.

Romans 4:18 (NIV)

Most of us want our faith to grow. The problem is that faith grows best when it is under trial, and very few people go out looking for trials and troubles just so their faith will increase.

Life is not always easy, nor does it always go the way we think it should. When life seems difficult or a situation seems impossible, God is waiting and willing to grow your faith.

Consider Romans 4:18-21 (NIV):

> *Against all hope, Abraham in hope believed and so became the father of many nations, just as it had been said to him, "So shall your offspring be." Without weakening in his faith, he faced the fact that his body was as good as dead—since he was about a hundred years old—and that Sarah's womb was also dead. Yet he did not waver through unbelief regarding the promise of God, but was strengthened in his faith and gave glory to God, being fully persuaded that God had power to do what he had promised.*

Against all hope, Abraham in hope believed.

It made no sense for Abraham to believe he would be a daddy. He was 100 years old, for crying out loud! And Sarah—Sarah was 90. Who in the world would ever think a 90-year-old chick would have a baby?

Against all hope, Abraham in hope believed.

The parts that needed to work in order for Abraham and Sarah to have a baby had long since been retired from use.

Against all hope, Abraham in hope believed.

It made no sense that Sarah would be having morning sickness or looking for maternity clothes, yet Abraham believed.

Do you want to be an "against all hope" follower of Christ? Do you want so to believe that your God is able to bring about the impossible or unlikely in your life that others just look at you and shake their heads?

If God clues you in on something He wants to do in and through you, have faith and believe, no matter how unlikely it is that it will happen.

Against all hope, _____
(insert your name), in hope, believed.

Hebrews 12:2

Let us fix our eyes on Jesus, the author and perfecter of our faith, who for the joy set before him endured the cross, scorning its shame, and sat down at the right hand of the throne of God.

Hebrews 12:2 (NIV)

Fix Your Eyes On JESUS!

Not on the marriage in trouble,

...the person speaking ill of you,

...the illness taking your health,

...the aging of your body,

...the emptiness of your bank account,

...the waywardness of your child,

...the evil abounding in our world,

...the economy,

...the exam you will take,

...or any one of a thousand other things that vie for your attention.

NO!!

Fix your eyes on Jesus.

It is only in the fixing of your eyes on the One who controls the winds and the waves, the One who created us and loves us more than we can ever imagine....

It is only when you stare steadily at Him and allow Him to lead you and guide you that you will know joy and peace, even in the midst of a world that seems to be spinning out of control.

So, friend, fix your eyes on Jesus and trust His heart completely.

Jeremiah 32:17

Ah Lord GOD! Behold, You have made the heavens and the earth by Your great power and by Your outstretched arm! Nothing is too difficult for You.

Jeremiah 32:17 (NASB)

When was the last time you were walking through a situation in your life where you just wanted to put your hands on your hips in a show of defiance and shout to the heavens, "But God, it's too hard. I can't do it."

Did you know that our heavenly Father, who created the heavens and earth by His mighty power and outstretched arm, never comes up against something that is too hard for Him? He never experiences angst or fear over a situation. He never thinks, "It is too hard. I can't do it." Never!

Whatever situation you are in right now, be encouraged to know that it is not too big / hard / difficult / painful / awkward / uncomfortable for God to handle. If God can create every intricate detail of this world and the world beyond, including you, know that He is able to handle your problems and concerns. Even though the situation might feel too hard for you, nothing is too hard for God.

Isaiah 43:2

Have you ever known someone who is walking through horrific personal circumstances, yet endures gracefully? Perhaps this describes your situation, or maybe you don't feel like you are enduring very well at all, and certainly not gracefully.

Is your heart so hurt that you think it might never recover? Do the hurt and tears threaten to overwhelm you every moment of every day? Has your world fallen apart?

Listen! Can you hear your God whispering to you?

> *When you go through deep waters, I will be with you. When you go through rivers of difficulty, you will not drown. When you walk through the fire of oppression, you will not be burned up; the flames will not consume you.*
>
> Isaiah 43:2 (NLT)

Do you feel God's presence in your situation? Can you walk a bit more confidently, knowing that you are not alone? God promises you will not be consumed by this trial. Hear the love in His voice as He says, "I will be with you…whatever the situation, I am here."

One thing you can count on, dear one. God always keeps His promises. Always.

James 1:1

Take a look at James 1:1 (NIV):

James, a servant of God and of the Lord Jesus Christ, To the twelve tribes scattered among the nations; Greetings.

It's a greeting, right? Nothing special here. Wrong!!

James had bragging rights as the half brother of Jesus. He was a leader in the early church. Yet, here he is voluntarily calling himself a servant of God and of the Lord Jesus Christ.

We live in a very ME-oriented society. When was the last time you put yourself in the role of a servant? Have you washed any feet lately? Spent your money on the poor instead of yourself? When was the last time you were treated like a servant? How do you react when someone treats you like a slave or servant?

It is easy to talk of being a servant of Christ, but do you live out that role?

Do you feed the poor, care for widows, tell others about Jesus, show mercy to those who need it, and love those who are different from you? Jesus told us to do all of that. He bought and paid for us with His blood, so He owns us. Do you always do what Jesus asks?

Romans 8:18

The days in which we live seem to bring almost constant accounts of sickness, destruction, tragedy, and loss. Hurricanes, earthquakes, tornados, cancer, marriages crumbling, children going astray, jobs lost, human trafficking, and so much more. The list of suffering and troubles seems endless.

The apostle Paul knew a bit about suffering. He experienced multiple beatings, stoning, being shipwrecked and lost at sea, being robbed, imprisoned, hungry, cold, naked, and snakebit, being scorned by his own people and so much more—all for the sake of spreading the gospel of Jesus Christ.

Yet, in spite of all he suffered, he said something so significant in Romans 8:18 (NKJV):

For I consider that the sufferings of this present time are not worthy to be compared with the glory which shall be revealed in us.

Can you go there with Paul? Whatever you suffer now, in this life, will pale in comparison to the glory, the awesomeness, of what awaits you in heaven. It is not always easy to walk out that belief in the midst of trials.

Paul encourages you to think bigger…broader…beyond NOW. He wants you to see your life through heavenly eyes. One day that won't be so difficult. One day you will look in the rearview mirror and understand that what overwhelms you now was used by God to bring you one step closer to Him…one step nearer heaven.

Until then, you walk by faith and not by sight. Trust Him and walk with Him through this life. One day you will walk from this life right on into the next, and then your mouth will fly open, your eyes will be as wide as saucers and you will say, "NOW, I understand."

Psalm 46:10

Be still, and know that I am God; I will be exalted among the nations, I will be exalted in the earth.

Psalm 46:10 (NKJV)

Be still and know…that God is in control and knows the plan.

Be still and know…that God knows your anxieties.

Be still and know…that God is never anxious.

Be still and know…that if you seek God, you will find Him.

Be still and know…that He was not taken surprise with the diagnosis the doctor gave.

Be still and know…that the political problems of the world do not cause God one moment of angst.

Be still and know…that God knows all about your financial trouble.

Be still and know…that God will walk with you into old age.

Be still and know…that just because things don't turn out the way you thought they would does not mean all is lost.

Be still and know…that when He wants you to walk in a new direction, you will be the first to know about it.

Be still and know…that God is trustworthy and faithful.

Be still and know…that He has your back.

Be still and know…that He sings over you and delights in you…YES, YOU!!!

Be still and know…that He has a plan for you.

Be still and know…that He is enough for whatever you are going through.

Be still and know…that NOTHING is too hard for God.

When you fix your focus on God, you can find peace and calm, and yes, even contentment in the midst of your days.

Isaiah 46:4

God may very well be partial to older folks—not that He doesn't like young people, mind you. He does. But think about how often in the Bible, God used someone of advanced age to accomplish something BIG.

- Noah was over 500 years old when he built the ark.
- Abraham was 100 years old when Isaac was born.
- Joseph was middle aged when he saved his family from the famine.
- Moses was 80ish when he led the Israelites out of Egypt.
- Joshua was almost 90 when he became the leader of the Israelites and led them to the Promised Land.
- David was in his final years when he amassed the materials for Solomon to use in building the magnificent temple of God.

- **Paul had graduated from seminary and moved up in the ranks of the Pharisees before he came to know Jesus. He was no spring chicken.**

It seems pretty clear that God has a special affinity for those who have some gray in their hair. Someone once said, *"It is a shame youth is wasted on the young."* Most of us don't acquire any measure of wisdom until we have walked more than a few miles on this dusty earth and made a whole passel of mistakes from which we hopefully learn.

Consider this verse from Isaiah:

> *Even to your old age and gray hairs I am he, I am he who will sustain you. I have made you and I will carry you; I will sustain you and I will rescue you.*
>
> Isaiah 46:4 (NIV)

God esteems older folks and wants them to know that He values them.

2 Corinthians 1:3-4

There is a reason for your today.

Are times good for you right now? **There is a reason.**

Are you walking through a trial in this season? **There is a reason**.

Are your circumstances vastly different than you had hoped or dreamed they would be? **There is a reason.**

In fact, there probably are many reasons. God is not required to limit Himself to one reason for allowing things into our lives. He works ALL things out, in many ways, for many reasons, for those whose hearts are sold out to Him.

Today, however, it is important to understand that whatever you are going through may very well also be for the benefit of someone else. Perhaps you cannot see or even begin to understand how in the world your situation could be for someone else's benefit. For heaven's sake, it doesn't even seem to be for *your* benefit right now. Walk this one out in faith, dear one.

Be reminded of Paul's words in 2 Corinthians 1: 3-4 (NCV)

> *Praise be to the God and Father of our Lord Jesus Christ. God is the Father who is full of mercy and all comfort. He comforts us every time we have trouble, so when others have trouble, we can comfort them with the same comfort God gives us.*

One day, God will place someone in your life with a trial similar to yours. In that moment, you will be able to comfort her because of your experiences. Know that God never wastes a trial in your life. He always draws a beautiful circle of comfort.

2 Timothy 2:13

How often do you mess up?

How often **today** did you mess up?

You may need fingers and toes to count the times you said or did or thought something that was not high on God's list of things that please Him.

Impatience, irritability, selfishness, pride—**all before 8 a.m.**

Do you find that some days are better than others? You might not need that extra hand to count on until, say, after noon. But other days faithfulness just is not happening.

Have you ever wondered if God has the urge to throw up His holy hands and say, *"I give up on her. She is such a screw up. Why can't she get it right?"*

How about some good news?

> *If we are unfaithful, he remains faithful, for he cannot deny who he is.*
>
> 2 Timothy 2:13 (NLT)

Your faithfulness, or lack thereof, does not change Who God is one iota. He is still the unchanging, faithful God who looked down across the millennia, saw you living out your life, and said, *"That one right there is gonna need Me to be faithful, because there will be times she will completely lose her way. That one…I love her so."*

Because of God's covenant love for you, He keeps His promises to you.

Because of God's covenant love for you, He remains true to Who He is…

Jehovah Shalom—The Lord Our Peace

Jehovah Rapha—The Lord Our Healer

El Shaddai—The All-Sufficient One

Jehovah Shammah—The Lord Is There

El Elyon—God Most High

Yahweh Ra'ah—The Lord My Shepherd

Prince of Peace

Creator

Redeemer

Abba, Daddy

He remains faithful!

Matthew 1:5-6

Think you've made a mess of your life?

Not sure if God even knows you are alive, much less wants to be your friend?

Let's look at the following verses from Matthew 1:5-6 (NASB) and learn a bit about the heart of God:

> *Salmon was the father of Boaz by Rahab, Boaz was the father of Obed by Ruth, and Obed the father of Jesse. Jesse was the father of David the king. David was the father of Solomon by Bathsheba who had been the wife of Uriah.*

Rahab…you know her, the prostitute. She was the mother of a godly man of character named Boaz.

Boaz married Ruth, a foreigner, a non-Israelite… considered to be unclean by the Israelites. Could it be that Boaz had learned unconditional love from a mother who had never known it until she met the God of Israel?

Ruth was the grandmother of King David—the greatest king Israel ever knew. In spite of his moral failure with Bathsheba, David was a man after God's own heart.

Bathsheba—the *other* woman with whom David committed adultery—the wife of Uriah, one of David's mighty men. She was the mother of Solomon, the wisest man ever to live.

If you continue reading in Matthew 1, you eventually come to the end of the genealogy and find the final name is JESUS. Three women who seemed like the most unlikely candidates to be used by God—three women who were the great, great, greats of our Lord, Jesus Christ.

Think you've made an irretrievable mess of your life?

Rahab, Ruth, and Bathsheba would argue that you are exactly where God wants you. They are proof that God forgives, redeems, and restores. All you have to do is run to Him.

Luke 5:5

Lord, what You are asking me to do makes absolutely no sense.

I know to you it doesn't, My child.

So why don't we do it a different way, Lord?

I have My reasons.

And…You are not going to tell me what the reasons are?

Not right now, but eventually you will know.

So, until then, I just do it Your way and trust that it will all work out?

You got it! That's what faith is all about. Oh, and by the way, you are not the first to walk this path.

I'm not?

No, there was this disciple named Peter who had to learn this very same lesson…and learn he did, right out in the middle of the Sea of Galilee.

"But Simon answered and said to Him, 'Master we have toiled all night and caught nothing; nevertheless at Your word I will let down the net.'"

    Luke 5:5 (NKJV)

You see, my child, it is all about what you do with the "nevertheless." Nevertheless could be followed by, "I'll trust myself and do it my own way, Lord" or by "I'll trust You and do it Your way, Lord."

It's all about what comes after the "nevertheless."

Psalm 87:6

Feeling alone?

Abandoned? Forsaken? Forgotten?

Like no one cares or even knows you exist on this spinning ball called earth?

Perhaps the phone has not rung in days. Maybe the text messages have stopped coming. It could even be that your best friend seems to have found other company.

The loneliness is unbearable and the silence is deafening.

Where is everyone? Is there anyone out there or are you alone in this world?

Suddenly, a knock comes on the door of your heart.

Who is it?

It is Jesus and He has a message for you.

> *The Lord will record, when He registers the peoples: "This one was born there."*
>
> Psalm 87:6 (NKJV)

God knows where you were born! Nation, state, city, town, hospital, right down to which bassinet you were placed in for visitors to ooh and aah over.

He knows, and what's more, He wrote it down. So, if He knows all that about your beginning, don't you think He knows where you are right now?

By the way, maybe He is just waiting for you to invite Him into your world for a cup of coffee and a chat.

Proverbs 8:17

I love those who love me, And those who seek me diligently will find me.

Proverbs 8:17 (NKJV)

Two things are promised in this verse. Two very important things: God's love and His presence. To have one without the other is to settle for less. Think about it.

To possess God's love without His Presence puts you in the same predicament as the Israelites after they worshiped the golden calf.

God, in total exasperation, told Moses He would send the Israelites, His chosen people whom He loved, into the Promised Land, but His Presence would not go with them.

For Moses, the Presence of God was a non-negotiable. He knew the Israelites must have God's Presence, not just His love, in order to be set apart. There would be no relationship between God and His chosen people without His Presence.

God's Love + God's Presence = RELATIONSHIP

Do you feel you have lost God's Presence or love? God has not stopped giving; He gives generously to those who seek Him. Yet, He requires that you love Him and seek Him.

1 Thessalonians 5:18

Corrie ten Boom tells the story of her time in the Nazi concentration camp Ravensbrück. She and her sister, Betsie, were subjected to horrific conditions and treatment during their time there. They lived, along with 1400 other women, in a flea- and lice-infested dormitory designed for 400 occupants. There were less than 10 toilets to accommodate the women and usually they were stopped up and overflowing with raw sewage. The women were starved, beaten, and worked in deplorable situations for 11 hours each day.

Corrie and Betsie were Christians who had been able, by God's grace, to smuggle a Bible into the camp. One of the first days they were incarcerated they opened the Scripture to 1 Thessalonians 5: 18. Betsie read this verse to Corrie:

> *Be thankful in all circumstances, for this is God's will for you who belong to Christ Jesus.*
>
> 1 Thessalonians 5:18 (NLT)

Betsie was insistent they obey. They thanked God that they had been able to stay together, that they had been able to smuggle their Bible in, and that they had not been killed. They thanked God that they were able to share the gospel through their nightly Bible study and prayer times with many in the dormitory who became Christians. They thanked God that the guards seemed to stay away from their dormitory, which gave them much more freedom than other dormitories experienced. They thanked God for many things during those dark and dreadful days.

One day Betsie insisted they thank God for the fleas. This was too much for Corrie. She protested mightily. The fleas and lice were constantly causing them misery and disease. How could she thank God for the fleas? Finally, she agreed to thank God for the fleas and did so regularly.

After months in Ravensbrück, Betsie overheard the guards talking. What she heard astounded her. The reason she and Corrie had such freedom to share the gospel in the dormitory was because none of the guards would come into the building

BECAUSE OF THE FLEAS. The fleas had saved the lives of Corrie and Betsie and allowed them to share Jesus with untold numbers of women.

Are you thankful in ALL circumstances? Are there "fleas" in your life for which you need to thank God? He may very well be using those "fleas" for your good. Thank Him for them today.

Joshua 9:14

Decisions, decisions.

Sometimes they are clear-cut and can be made easily.

Other times…not so much.

Some people make decisions by weighing the evidence for and against the decision and then make a choice based on all the information. Other folks just go with gut instinct. There is, however, a third and much better option.

Joshua and the Israelites learned about this option the hard way. They were in a position to decide whether or not to make a treaty with the Gibeonites. The Gibeonites *said* they were from a far country. Their evidence *seemed* to confirm many days, even months, of travel to arrive at the place where the Israelites camped. Joshua 9:14 (NCV) tells us how Israel made their decision:

> *The men of Israel tasted the bread, but they did not ask the Lord what to do.*

Joshua and the leaders considered the evidence being offered by the Gibeonites, who, by the way, tricked them. The evidence was convincing and the Israelites fell for it.

Why? They did not ask the Lord what to do. They failed to get God's opinion. God had already told Israel decades before not to make a treaty with any of the inhabitants of the land, but Joshua failed to consult God. Because of this failure to ask God what He desired, the Israelites were locked into a treaty that would be like a noose around their necks for generations.

What decision do you have to make today? Have you considered the evidence but forgotten to ask God's opinion? STOP NOW! Ask the Lord what His desire is in the situation. In doing so, you will guarantee yourself not only a good decision, but a God-decision.

Job 13:15

God: *Do you trust Me?*

You: Me? Do I trust You? Well, of course, I do.

God: *How much do you trust Me?*

You: I trust You completely, Lord.

God: *Really? Do you trust Me with your marriage?*

You: Sure I do.

God: *Then why are you always trying to change your husband?*

You: Well, umm, maybe I need a little work on that. But, he needs to change.

God: *Hmmm, he's not the only one. Do you trust Me with your money?*

You: I tithe, don't I? That should count.

God: *Yes, you do and that does count, but do you give until it hurts or just until it pinches a bit?*

You: I could give more. I will give more!

God: *Do you trust Me with your health? What if I allowed you to be diagnosed with cancer or*

some other devastating disease? Would you trust Me then?

You: Wow! Lord, that's pretty heavy. I can't understand why You would allow that. It doesn't seem like it would work out too well. Surely You wouldn't do that at my age. I'm still young and I've got lots of life left to live.

God: *I'm not saying I am going to do that. I'm just asking would you still trust Me if I did OR if I allowed it to happen to your child?*

You: _____
_____
_____

Do you trust God with everything and in all situations? Can you echo Job's words from Job 13:15 (NKJV):

Though He slay me, yet will I trust Him.

Do you have a "though He slay me, yet will I trust Him" kind of faith?

Luke 19:5

Hey, you!

Those are not exactly words of intimacy and friendship. There is nothing personal about someone saying, "Hey you!"

"Hey you" could be directed at anyone, anywhere. It is a greeting that would likely come from a complete stranger and probably would not be followed by something that really warmed your heart.

Do you feel your life is one "Hey you" moment after another? Are you convinced that no one knows your name or cares very much about you? Has it been a while since your telephone rang and a friendly voice spoke your name in a caring way? Have the cards and letters with the beautiful *Dear*_____ greeting ceased to show up in your mailbox? Are you convinced there is an *I am nobody, please ignore me* sign emblazoned on your forehead?

Would you like a bit of good news from another soul who thought he was unnoticed?

When Jesus came by, he looked up at Zacchaeus and called him by name. "Zacchaeus!" he said. "Quick, come down! For I must be a guest in your home today."

Luke 19:5 (NLT)

Zacchaeus was a hated Jewish tax collector. No one wanted to be friends with him. No one cared about him because he had not been much of a friend to anyone in a very long time. He lived a lonely existence outside of his interactions with other tax collectors.

But Jesus knew his name. Jesus called to him by name.

Zacchaeus!!

Not "Hey you!" *Zacchaeus!! Hurry up, get down here. I need to visit your house.*

Friend, Jesus knows your name and He is calling out to you because He wants to visit with you today. Listen! Hear Him calling your name?

Psalm 91:1-2

Where are you living?

Not the town or city of your physical address, but rather the address of your heart. Where does your heart abide?

"Home is where the heart is," and home is where most of us find safety and security.

Is your life calm or do you find a great deal of unrest in your heart at the moment? Are your emotions whirling around without finding a peaceful spot on which to rest? Are you looking for shelter from the raging storms of life?

> *Those who live in the shelter of the Most High will find rest in the shadow of the Almighty. This I declare of the LORD: He alone is my refuge, my place of safety; he is my God, and I trust him.*
>
> Psalm 91:1-2 (NLT)

The shelter provided by God, the Most High God, is the place where you will find rest, refuge, and safety. He stands in the door, beckoning you to enter, to take off the cloak of anxiety and lay down your load of care and worry. You have an open invitation from the One who controls the wind and the waves, to make His shelter the address for your heart. Do you trust Him enough to enter and abide?

2 Chronicles 20:12

O our God, will You not judge them? For we have no power against this great multitude that is coming against us; nor do we know what to do, but our eyes are upon You.

2 Chronicles 20:12 (NKJV)

What does the *multitude* that is coming against you look like? You may not have a huge army advancing toward you like the ancient Israelites did, but your *multitude* is just as real and just as frightening.

Your *multitude* may be a cancer diagnosis, a foreclosure notice, a pink slip from your job, or a spouse's words, "I just don't love you anymore." Any of these would surely feel like a *multitude* coming against you.

A wayward child, the death of a loved one, or perhaps just a usual day's worth of worries and troubles piled on top of those from previous days—a *multitude* can take many forms. Just because one person's multitude seems trivial to another makes it no less a *multitude* for the soul watching it advance.

So, what do you do about this great *multitude* coming against you? The magnitude of it is too large for you to truly do much about it in your own strength. You cannot see how you can stand against this. Do what the Israelites did. Do what hundreds and thousands who have gone before you have done.

Shift your gaze from the *multitude* onto the One who is able to do something about it. Focus your eyes on God. Resist the urge to allow the *multitude* to be your object of focus. Instead, fix your eyes and heart on God. He has the power to deal with whatever is pressing in upon you. He is able to deliver you from—or through—that *multitude*. Make a choice to place your eyes on Him.

Psalm 139:13-14

The southeastern portion of the United States is green and lush with many different varieties of grass, trees, and plants. Even in the winter, there is a portion of green, compliments of evergreens like the pine tree. Spring and summer bring a profusion of color…blooms of white, red, purple, yellow, and blue…surrounded by a background of deep green. Autumn foliage offers leaf watchers delight after colorful delight with every shade of yellow, red, orange, and brown imaginable.

By contrast, the desert southwest is vastly different. The soil is dry and sandy with a profusion of rocks and a scarcity of green grass. The plants are leggy and prickly, yet beautiful with muted shades of green and brown. The stately saguaro cacti dot the landscape, standing tall and straight. In the summer, many of the cacti proffer delightful blooms of red and yellow.

Two different regions of the country boasting two unique landscapes—both are beautiful. Neither is wrong or bad. God made them both with purpose and intent.

Why can we celebrate and enjoy the differences in landscape, but not in our bodies? God created each of us unique, different. Tall and short; black, white, or yellow; faces round, thin, or long; blondes, red heads, brunettes, or bald; thin and not-so-thin; different personalities—serious, funny, melancholy, quiet, or boisterous. Each of us is different. Stop being so critical and dissatisfied with God's creation. Instead, celebrate your uniqueness. You are exactly who God intended you to be!!

You made all the delicate, inner parts of my body and knit me together in my mother's womb. Thank you for making me so wonderfully complex! Your workmanship is marvelous—how well I know it.

Psalm 139:13-14 (NLT)

2 Corinthians 4:1

You have work to do! You have ministry to do!

Your work is not the same as your friend's work or your neighbor's work. Your ministry is unique and appointed to you by God. Perhaps it involves raising children or caring for aging parents. It might involve being a light for Christ in the workplace where you stand as the lone Christian. Your work may be church or ministry related, but it also might involve making home a safe and loving harbor for your family. Your ministry may bring you in contact with the sick and hurting or the well and whole. It could be ministry to the one or to the masses.

Wherever God has placed you in this season of your life is where your ministry is to be done. Home. Church. Workplace. Gym. Daycare. Hospital. School. Doctor's office. Deer stand. 18-wheeler. Nursing home. Wherever you are is where you have work to do for God's kingdom.

Don't like where you are in this season? Are you dealing with uncertainty and confusion about your work and ministry? Is the path ahead foggy and fraught with potholes?

You are not alone. Apparently Paul's path was rife with the same barriers. Be encouraged by Paul's words:

> *Therefore, since we have this ministry [work], as we have received mercy, we do not lose heart.*
>
> 2 Corinthians 4:1 (NKJV) *emphasis added*

As a follower of Christ your work is your ministry, and God, in His mercy and kindness, has allowed you unique opportunities to participate in His work. So, friend, do not lose heart. Stay the course. Be faithful to the last word you heard God speak into your heart.

Do not lose heart! Do not lose hope!

Daniel 2:20-22

Praise the name of God forever and ever, for he has all wisdom and power. He controls the course of world events; he removes kings and sets up other kings. He gives wisdom to the wise and knowledge to the scholars. He reveals deep and mysterious things and knows what lies hidden in darkness, though he himself is surrounded by light.

Daniel 2:20-22 (NLT)

Look again at those verses and take in everything they tell you about the God you serve:

- He has *all* wisdom.
- He has *all* power.
- He controls what takes place in the world.
- He decides who sits in the seat of power in nations around the world.
- He gives His wisdom to all who desire to be wise.

- He gives His knowledge to those who seek after knowledge.
- He gives man understanding about all sorts of mysteries.
- He knows what kind of monsters hide in our dark places.

Does that sound like an out-of-control God? Does that sound like a God who has abandoned His creation? No!

Today, dear one, be encouraged that your God is in control of a world that seems to be spinning out of control. He is handling the mysteries and monsters that seek to weaken your faith. Trust Him and praise the name of God forever and ever.

Revelation 2:17

When was the last time you heard your name spoken with tenderness and love? Perhaps it was as recently as a few minutes ago, but for some it might have been years.

Your name is personal and the calling out of it evokes strong responses in your heart. Consider some situations where your name might be called out:

- The classroom
- The physician's office
- A contest
- A telephone call
- A chance meeting
- A parent or other authority figure

Each of those scenarios, where your name might be called out, brings forth different emotional responses based on your life experiences. In some of these situations, your name might have been called out harshly or with condemnation, while in others your name was voiced tenderly, with kindness. At times the calling out of your name could cause anxiety or fear, while other times your spoken name brought forth feelings of love and safety.

One day, if you are a believer in Jesus Christ, you will receive a new name. It will not be a name that has negative connotations attached to it, nor will it be a name that anyone else knows. It will be uniquely yours, given to you by the One who loved you enough to die for you; a secret name between you and the Lover of your soul.

> *To him who overcomes I will give some of the hidden manna to eat. And I will give him a white stone, and on the stone a new name written which no one knows except him who receives it.*
>
> Revelation 2:17 (NKJV)

A new name. *Your* new name given to you by Jesus. Hold on, precious one, your new name will be wonderful.

Philippians 4:11

How do you score on the contentment scale?

Zero to ten with zero being "not at all content" and ten being "totally content". Where do you fall on the scale?

Does your contentment score change with the changing seasons and circumstances of life, or are you at the same level of contentment most of the time? Perhaps you are one of those blessed ones who are content with the life God has assigned you. You trust His heart in whatever situation comes your way and rarely complain. Unfortunately, there are not many of those around. Most people are given to complaining and discontent when life doles out a heaping helping of trial and testing.

Paul, the apostle who experienced the highest highs and the lowest lows as he ministered for Christ had this to say about contentment:

> *Not that I speak in regard to need, for I have learned in whatever state I am, to be content.*
>
> Philippians 4:11 (NKJV)

How did he do that? How do you do it?

The answer comes in Philippians 4:13 (NKJV):

> *I can do all things through Christ who strengthens me.*

When you take life's highest highs and lowest lows, not in your own strength, but in the strength of Jesus, you too, will score a ten on the contentment scale. Shift your focus off your circumstances and onto Jesus, and you will be content.

Psalm 17:8

Keep me as the apple of your eye; hide me in the shadow of your wings.

Psalm 17:8 (ESV)

The eye—one of the most sensitive parts of the body—something in your eye that does not belong is removed quickly. Eye protection is key to good vision and good health.

In Psalm 17:8, the psalmist is asking the Lord to protect him in the same way you would protect your eye. In essence, the psalmist cries out to God, asking for protection in the midst of trial and trouble. An analogy—consider that David is asking for Secret Service protection, the best of the best.

How often have you flippantly flung prayers for protection heavenward? When was the last time you asked God to protect you; to hide you; to be your heavenly Secret Service detail? Dear one, you are his precious child and He takes care of you in the same tender manner in which you care for your eye. Trust Him.